Contents

Water for life

Water! What would we do without it? We wash, cook and clean with it and drink it by the glass. But none of us should ever take water for granted. Like every animal and plant on Earth, we could not live without it.

Water is a **liquid** with no colour, taste or smell. Yet without it we could not survive.

You need to drink plenty of water to keep your body working properly.

Save the Planet

Stop Water Waste

Claire Llewellyn

Chrysalis Children's Books

First published in the UK in 2003 by
Chrysalis Children's Books
An imprint of Chrysalis Books Group Plc
The Chrysalis Building
Bramley Road
London W10 6SP

Paperback edition first published in 2005

ISBN 1-84138-693-6 (hb)
ISBN 1-84458-303-1 (pb)

British Library Cataloguing in Publication Data for this book is available from the British Library.

Editorial Manager: Joyce Bentley
Senior Editor: Sarah Nunn
Design: Stonecastle Graphics Ltd
Illustrations: Paul B. Davies
Picture researcher: Paul Turner

Printed in China

10 9 8 7 6 5 4 3 2 1

Picture credits:
Corbis:
pages 1 © Chinch Gryniewicz; Ecoscene/Corbis, 21 (top) © Corbis.
Garden & Wildlife Matters Photo Library:
pages 5 © M.Collins/Garden Matters (below centre), 14 © Wildlife Matters, 15 © Wildlife Matters (top), 16 © Garden Matters (right), 21 (below).
Roddy Paine Photographic Studios:
pages 4, 5 (top), 15 (below), 26-27, 28.
Stonecastle Graphics:
pages 7 (top), 16 (left).
Sylvia Cordaiy Photo Library:
pages 17 (left), 19 (below).

◄ Plants contain a lot of water. All of them need water to grow.

Animals cannot survive without water. They will travel a long way to find it. ▼

The Earth's water

Large parts of the Earth are covered with water, but only some of it is good to drink. The water we use has to be fresh. **Fresh water** is found in rivers and lakes or deep under the ground.

Water covers a lot of the Earth's surface, but sea water is no good to us. It is much too salty to drink.

Fresh water is the only water ▶
we can drink. Some of it is
found in rivers like this.

Fresh water is precious. There is
very little of it on Earth. Most of
the Earth's fresh water is locked
in ice at the Poles. ▼

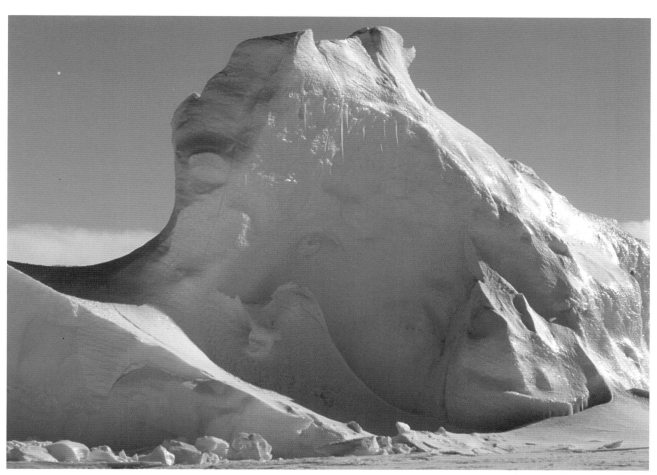

The water cycle

Water on Earth is always on the move – from the sea to the air and back to the land. This movement is called the **water cycle**. Earth's water is **recycled** again and again, so it is important to keep it clean.

The Sun heats the water in seas and lakes.

The water changes into a **gas** called **water vapour** and rises into the air.

The **water vapour** begins to cool as it rises. It changes back into tiny droplets of water and forms clouds.

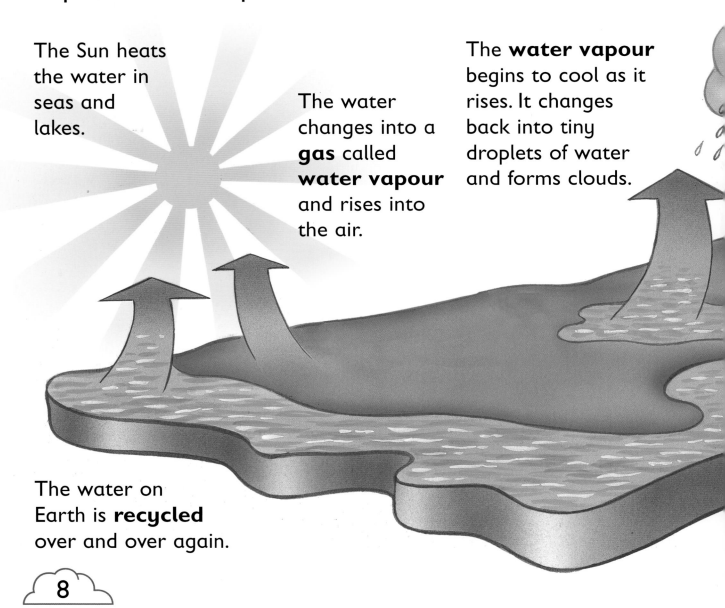

The water on Earth is **recycled** over and over again.

An oil tanker spills oil into the ocean harming animal and plant life.

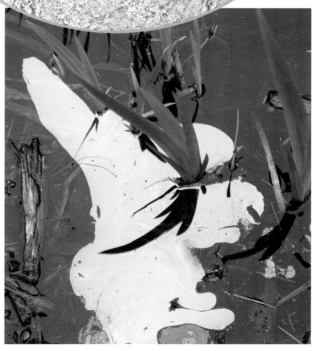

The water in the clouds falls to land as rain. It fills up rivers that flow to the sea.

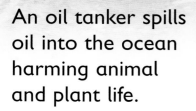

The water cycle is very important for life on Earth.

All of us need clean water. If we **pollute** rivers and seas, we are poisoning our **water supply**.

Getting rid of waste

It is easy to pollute the water supply. Many of us do it without even knowing it when we throw things away. Look closely at the picture below. Can you see how everyday waste pollutes rivers and streams?

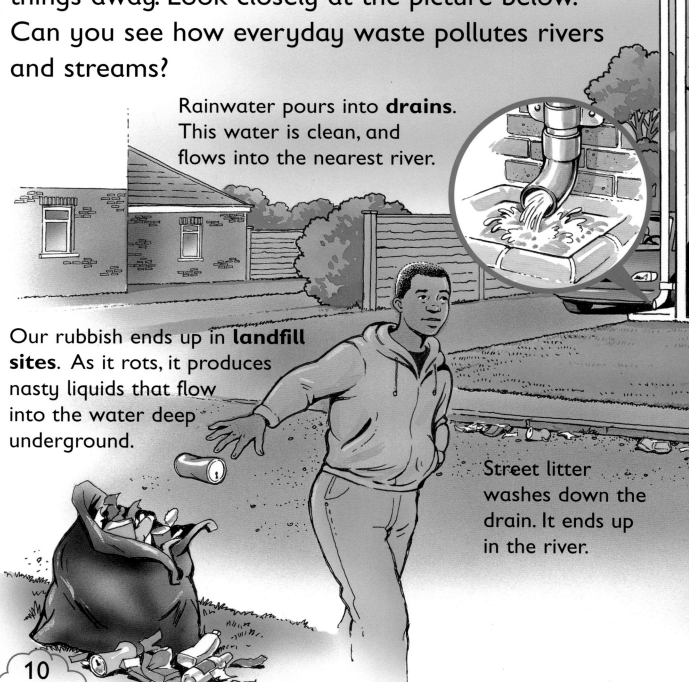

Rainwater pours into **drains**. This water is clean, and flows into the nearest river.

Our rubbish ends up in **landfill sites**. As it rots, it produces nasty liquids that flow into the water deep underground.

Street litter washes down the drain. It ends up in the river.

Rubbish is put down the toilet. It goes to **treatment plants**, which cannot cope with it.

Household cleaners are carried to the same treatment plants. They cannot remove all the chemicals.

Oil and paint are being poured down the drain. They will flow into a river, too.

Powders and sprays from the garden wash into drains or soak into the ground.

A better way with waste

We need to try and make less waste. We also need to stop waste polluting our water supply. Can you see ways of doing this in the picture below?

Ponds and rivers are protected and enjoyed.

Waste paper, glass, metals and plastics are all recycled. This cuts down on rubbish.

Litter is put in the bin. Now it won't wash down the drain.

Nappies and other rubbish is put in the bin – not down the toilet.

These cleaning products are kinder to the **environment**.

Home-made **compost** feeds the garden and does not pollute the water supply.

Paint and other dangerous waste is taken to the **waste dump** where it is collected and handled safely.

13

Factories and farms

Factories and farms pollute our water. Factories sometimes get rid of their waste by pouring it into rivers. Many farmers use powders and sprays on their land. These run into rivers on rainy days, and pollute the water.

The pollution in this water comes from the factory above. It is treating the river like a rubbish bin.

◀ The sprays and fertilizers that farmers use on their land often end up in streams. This spoils the water.

River water is cleaned before ▶ it reaches our homes but not everything can be removed.

Freshwater habitats

Rivers and lakes are important **habitats**, and are home to many animals and plants. Water pollution harms habitats. It can poison living things and help to spread disease. The wildlife in these places needs our protection.

Rivers are home to many animals, like these otters, and to plants. They need clean water to survive.

In every habitat big animals feed on smaller animals, and the smallest animals feed on plants. Each **species** is a link in the **food chain**.

When small creatures are poisoned ▶ by pollution, the larger animals that feed on them will be poisoned, too.

▲ Some people help to protect the environment by cleaning rivers and streams.

Pollution in the sea

The sea is also being polluted — by dirty rivers that flow into it and by ships that dump waste or spill sticky, black oil. Thousands of plants and animals live in the sea. They can all be harmed by dirty water.

When oil is spilled at sea, beaches are damaged or destroyed.

◄ An **oil spill** can kill thousands of creatures. Here, someone is cleaning a seabird, whose feathers have been coated in oil.

Polluted waters wash to every corner of the world. **Coral reefs** are shrinking every year. The tiny animals that build the reefs cannot survive in polluted waters. ▼

More and more water

Every year, we are using more water. Our water comes from **reservoirs** that are filled by rivers and lakes. They are growing shallower, and in time they could dry up. We have to find ways of using less water.

In some parts of the world, farmers are using more water to grow more crops.

In many countries, people have ▶
power showers, washing
machines and dishwashers.
These things use a lot of water.

Too much water is being taken
from this river. If the river dries
up, the wildlife will not survive. ▼

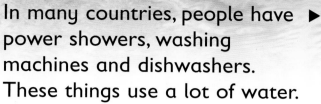

Using water

A leaking pipe, a running tap, an overflowing bucket… most of us waste water from time to time. Look carefully at the picture below. Can you see how water is being wasted?

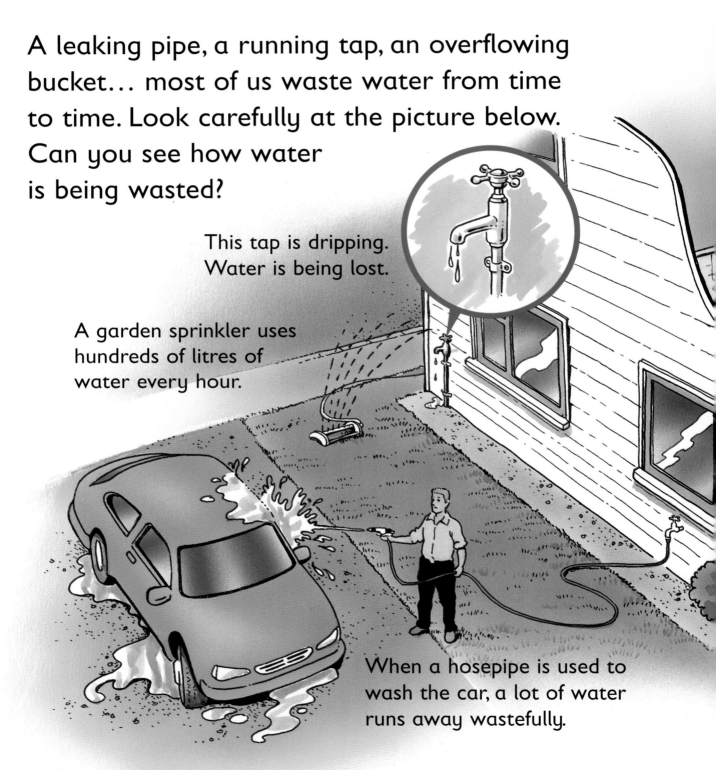

This tap is dripping. Water is being lost.

A garden sprinkler uses hundreds of litres of water every hour.

When a hosepipe is used to wash the car, a lot of water runs away wastefully.

A deep bath uses a lot of water.

Do you leave the tap running while you brush your teeth? That water is running away.

The dishwasher and washing machine use a lot of water. But they are running half-empty.

The water is left running until it's cold enough to drink.

A better way of using water

It's not hard to cut down on water waste. Look at the picture below. Can you see how people are saving water? If we save water, our reservoirs will be fuller, and lakes and rivers will be deeper, too.

Don't overwater the garden. Use a watering can when you do.

Only use your dishwasher and washing machine when they are full.

Turn taps off properly so they do not drip.

A short shower uses less water than a bath.

Turn the tap off when you wash your hands or brush your teeth.

Collect rainwater in a water barrel and use it to water the garden.

A bottle of water kept in the fridge is nice and cold to drink.

Small actions, big results

Is it possible for you to save water and fight water pollution? Of course, it is! And if your small steps are copied by millions of people, the results for the Earth will be huge! Everyone shares the planet and its water supply. Everyone can help to save it.

What would happen if everyone used water carefully?

We would take less water from rivers, lakes and streams. This would make them deeper, and any pollution in the water would be less strong.

These places would be safer habitats for wildlife.

There would be enough water for everyone to use.

What would happen if everyone stopped polluting rivers and the sea?

The water in rivers and lakes would be much cleaner. They would make better habitats for animals and plants.

Our drinking water would be safer.

The seas would be safe for swimmers, wildlife and underwater habitats, such as coral reefs.

Over to you!

Everyone wants plenty of clean, safe water. Why not try one of the ideas below, and help to stop pollution and water waste?

Talk to your parents about how you could save water at home. Look back at the ideas on pages 24-25.

Think of slogans to explain about pollution ("Don't dump down the drain") or encourage people to save water ("Be Water Wise"). Use them on posters to put up in your school, local library, club house or home.

Try and cut down on rubbish. For one week, keep a record of everything that's thrown away. What could have been recycled? Pin up your record for the family to see.

Recycle as much waste as you can. Encourage your family to have different bins to sort paper, glass, plastics, cans and compost.

Encourage your family to buy **organic** foods. Organic farming is kinder to the environment and does not use harmful powders and sprays.

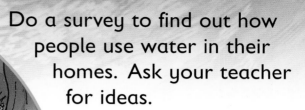

Do a survey to find out how people use water in their homes. Ask your teacher for ideas.

Investigate the way your school uses water. Make and display stickers and posters to encourage people to save water.

Older toilets use a lot of water. In many places you can get a simple device to put inside the **cistern** and save water.

Go pond- or stream-dipping with an adult. This is a good way to check on pollution. The cleaner the water, the more animals you'll find.

Be a 'friend' to local ponds and streams. If you see dead fish, a lot of rubbish or coloured water, contact the local water company.

Join a group in your area that helps to protect the environment. Some of the groups you could try are:

Friends of the Earth *www.foe.co.uk*
Greenpeace *www.greenpeace.org.uk*

Glossary

Cistern The water tank on a toilet.

Compost The crumbly mixture we add to soil to help plants to grow. Compost is made from rotted-down fruit and vegetable peelings.

Coral reef A long line of coral that lies under water in warm, shallow seas.

Drain A pipe that carries water away.

Environment The land, air and sea that make the world around us.

Food chain A way of showing what eats what in a habitat. Some animals feed on plants and are then eaten by other animals.

Fresh water The water that is found in rivers, lakes and under the ground. Fresh water is not salty, and is good to drink.

Gas A substance like air that is not solid or liquid. Air is made of a mixture of different gases.

Habitat The natural home of an animal or plant.

Landfill site A huge hole in the ground where rubbish is buried.

Liquid A substance like water that is runny.

Oil spill A large amount of oil that leaks onto land or into the sea.

Organic food Foods that have been grown in a natural way that is kinder to the environment.

Pollute To spoil the air, land or water with harmful things.

Recycle To make something new out of something old.

Reservoir A place where water is stored. Reservoirs look like huge lakes but they are built by people.

Species A kind of animal or plant.

Treatment plant A place where dirty water is cleaned.

Waste dump A place where people take rubbish that cannot be put in the bin.

Water cycle The movement of water from the sea into the air and back to the land.

Water supply All the water that people can use.

Water vapour Tiny droplets of water in air, which are so small you cannot see them.

Index

THE THREE LITTLE WOLVES
AND THE
BIG BAD PIG

EUGENE TRIVIZAS

ILLUSTRATED BY HELEN OXENBURY

EGMONT

For Grace
E.T.

In memory of
Stanley
H.O.

EGMONT
We bring stories to life

First published in Great Britain 1993
This edition published 2015
by Egmont UK Limited
The Yellow Building
1 Nicolas Road, London W11 4AN

www.egmont.co.uk

Once upon a time there were three cuddly little wolves with soft fur and fluffy tails who lived with their mother. The first was black, the second was grey and the third white.

One day the mother called the three little wolves round her and said, "My children, it is time for you to go out into the world. Go and build a house for yourselves. But beware of the big bad pig."

"Don't worry, Mother, we will watch out for him," said the three little wolves and they set off.

Soon they met a kangaroo who was pushing a
wheelbarrow full of red and yellow bricks.

"Please, will you give us some
of your bricks?" asked
the three little wolves.

"Certainly," said the kangaroo, and she gave them
lots of red and yellow bricks.

So the three little wolves built themselves a
house of bricks.

The very next day, the big bad pig came prowling
down the road and saw the house of bricks that
the little wolves had built.
  The three little wolves were playing croquet
in the garden. When they saw
the big bad pig coming,
they ran inside the house
and locked the door.

The pig knocked on the door and grunted,
   "Little wolves, little wolves, let me come in!"

"No, no, no," said the three little wolves. "By the
hair on our chinny-chin-chins, we will not let you
in, not for all the tea leaves in our china teapot!"

"Then I'll huff and I'll puff
and I'll blow your house down!"
said the pig.

So he huffed and he puffed
and he puffed and he huffed,
but the house didn't fall down.

But the pig wasn't called big and bad for nothing.
He went and fetched his sledgehammer and he
knocked the house down.

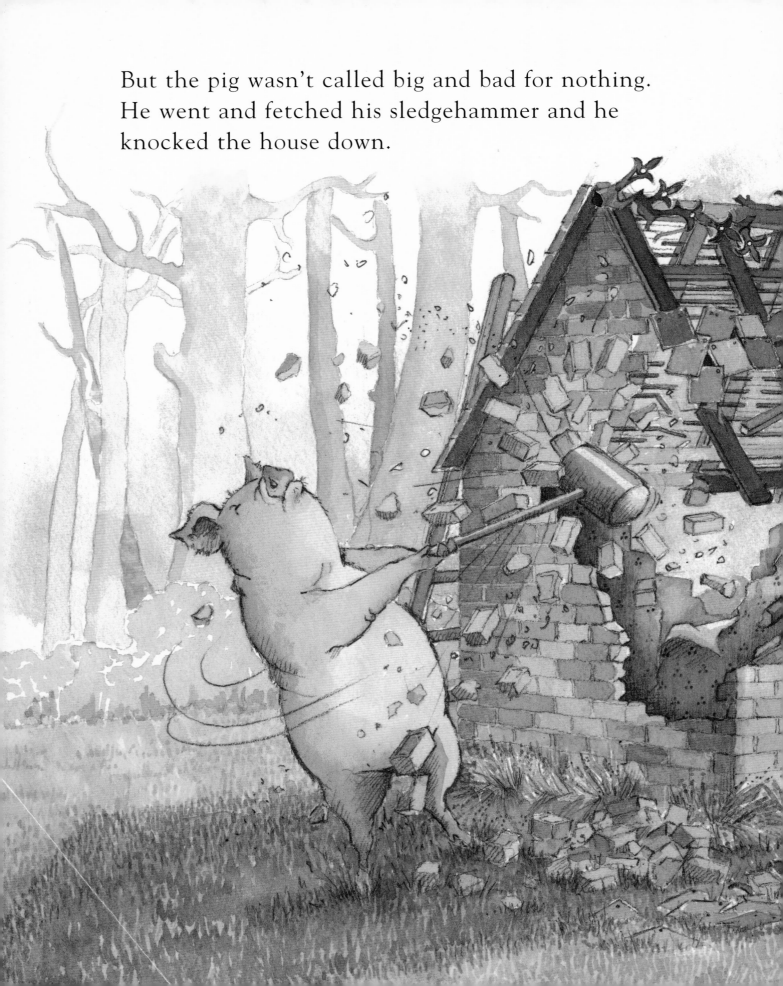

The three little wolves only
just managed to escape before the bricks
crumbled, and they were very frightened indeed.

"We shall have to build a stronger house," they said.
Just then, they saw a beaver who was mixing
concrete in a concrete mixer.

"Please, will you give us some of your concrete?"
asked the three little wolves.

"Certainly," said the beaver and he gave them buckets and buckets full of messy, slurry concrete.

So the three wolves built themselves a house of concrete.

No sooner had they finished than the big bad pig came prowling down the road and saw the house of concrete that the little wolves had built.

They were playing battledore and shuttlecock in the garden and when they saw the big bad pig coming, they ran inside their house and shut the door.

The pig rang the bell and said, "Little frightened wolves, let me come in!"

"No, no, no," said the three little wolves. "By the hair on our chinny-chin-chins, we will not let you in, not for all the tea leaves in our china teapot."

"Then I'll huff and I'll puff and I'll blow your house down!" said the pig.

So he huffed and he puffed and he puffed and he huffed, but the house didn't fall down.

But the pig wasn't called big and bad for nothing.
He went and fetched his pneumatic drill and
smashed the house down.

The three little wolves managed to escape but
their chinny-chin-chins were trembling and trembling
and trembling.

"We shall build an even stronger house," they said, because they were very determined. Just then, they saw a lorry coming along the road carrying barbed wire, iron bars, armour plates and heavy metal padlocks.

"Please, will you give us some of your barbed wire, a few iron bars and armour plates, and some heavy metal padlocks?" they said to the rhinoceros who was driving the lorry.

"Sure," said the rhinoceros and gave them plenty of barbed wire, iron bars, armour plates and heavy metal padlocks. He also gave them some plexiglass and some reinforced steel chains because he was a generous and kind-hearted rhinoceros.

So the three little wolves built themselves an extremely strong house. It was the strongest, securest house one could possibly imagine. They felt very relaxed and absolutely safe.

The next day, the big bad pig came prowling along
the road as usual. The little wolves were playing
hopscotch in the garden. When they saw the big bad
pig coming, they ran inside their house, bolted the
door and locked all the sixty-seven padlocks.

The pig pressed the video entrance phone and
said, "Frightened little wolves with the trembling
chins, let me come in!"

"No, no, no!" said the little wolves. "By the hair on our chinny-chin-chins, we will not let you in, not for all the tea leaves in our china teapot."

"Then I'll huff and I'll puff and I'll blow your house down!" said the pig.

So he huffed and he puffed and he puffed and he huffed, but the house didn't fall down.

But the pig wasn't called big and bad for nothing. He brought some dynamite, laid it against the house, lit the fuse and . . .

the house
blew up.

The little wolves
just managed to escape
with their fluffy tails scorched.

"Something must be wrong with our building materials," they said. "We have to try something different. But *what?*"

At that moment, they saw a flamingo bird coming along pushing a wheelbarrow full of flowers.

"Please, will you give us some flowers?" asked the little wolves.

"With pleasure," said the flamingo bird and gave them lots of flowers. So the three little wolves built themselves a house of flowers.

One wall was of marigolds, one wall of daffodils, one wall of pink roses and one wall of cherry blossom. The ceiling was made of sunflowers and the floor was a carpet of daisies. They had water lilies in their bathtub and buttercups in their fridge. It was a rather fragile house and it swayed in the wind, but it was very beautiful.

Next day, the big bad pig came prowling down the road and saw the house of flowers that the little wolves had built.

He rang the bluebell and said, "Little frightened wolves with the trembling chins and the scorched tails, let me come in!"

"No, no, no," said the three little wolves. "By the hair on our chinny-chin-chins, we will not let you in, not for all the tea leaves in our china teapot!"

"Then I'll huff and I'll puff and I'll blow your house down!" said the pig.

But as he took a deep breath, ready to huff and puff, he smelled the soft scent of the flowers. It was fantastic. And because the scent took his breath away, the pig took another breath and then another. Instead of huffing and puffing, he began to sniff.

He sniffed deeper and deeper until he was quite filled with the fragrant scent. His heart became tender and he realized how horrible he had been in the past. In other words, he became a big *good* pig. He started to sing and to dance the tarantella.

At first, the three little wolves were a bit worried, thinking that it might be a trick, but soon they realized that the pig had truly changed, so they came running out of the house. They introduced themselves and started playing games with him.

First they played pig-pog and then piggy-in-the-middle
and when they were all tired, they
invited him into the house.

They offered him china tea and strawberries
and wolfberries, and asked him to stay with
them as long as he wanted.
The pig accepted, and they all lived happily
together ever after.